IMAGES
of America

CARLISLE BARRACKS

On the cover: Please see page 106. (Courtesy U.S. Army Military History Institute.)

IMAGES
of America

CARLISLE BARRACKS

Roger S. Durham

ARCADIA
PUBLISHING

Copyright © 2009 by Roger S. Durham
ISBN 978-1-5316-4052-1

Published by Arcadia Publishing
Charleston, South Carolina

Library of Congress Control Number: 2008933609

For all general information contact Arcadia Publishing at:
Telephone 843-853-2070
Fax 843-853-0044
E-mail sales@arcadiapublishing.com
For customer service and orders:
Toll-Free 1-888-313-2665

Visit us on the Internet at www.arcadiapublishing.com

*Dedicated to the staff of the U.S. Army Heritage and Education Center,
who go beyond the call of duty every day to preserve the heritage of the
American soldier and help tell the army's story, one soldier at a time*

CONTENTS

ACKNOWLEDGMENTS

This book needed to be done, but I did not know I needed to do it. However, it was not something I could do by myself. The following are just a few of those who contributed, sometimes without their knowledge, and who helped make this happen: Col. Robert J. Dalessandro, the U.S. Army Heritage and Education Center's fearless leader; Col. J. Craig Nannos, friend, mentor, and entrepreneur; Dr. Conrad Crane, commander of the Military History Institute; Dr. Richard Sommers, scholar, historian, and Carlisle Barracks institution; Molly Bompane, master of the photograph collection; Greg Statler, the "Radar O'Reilly" of collections management; James McNally (thanks Jim, I could not have done it without you); Jay Graybeal, chief curator for the U.S. Army Heritage Museum and master of the monkey farm; Chris Semancik, "Captain Comet," ordnance master, and keeper of the guns; Paula Ussery, matriarch of the museum; Kaleb Dissinger, master technician and keeper of the homies; Ryan Meyer, master technician in training and Dissinger over-watch; Gary Johnson, master scanner and colleague; John Giblin, commander of visitor and education services; and the staff, faculty, and garrison of Carlisle Barracks and the U.S. Army War College.

A special vote of thanks goes to my wife, JoAnn, and daughters Star and Lacy, who once again put up with my clutter on the kitchen table and in the computer room, my lack of focus, distracted attention, and being hauled around while I took photographs. Their patience is beyond measure but appreciated more than I can express in words.

I would also like to extend my thanks to the following institutions for their assistance and donation of materials for this book: the U.S. Army Heritage and Education Center (USAHEC), the U.S. Army Military History Institute (USAMHI), the U.S. Army Heritage Museum (USAHM), the Library of Congress, and the Cumberland County Historical Society.

INTRODUCTION

In 1757, the world was at war. England and France were involved in a global conflict over land in the New World and whose influence would dominate. In North America, the British colonies on the East Coast found themselves being isolated from the territories to the west by the French in Canada who were cultivating influence with the Native Americans and establishing posts through the Ohio Valley and down the Mississippi River. Britain objected to this because it also infringed upon land that it claimed. The confluence of the Allegheny and Monongahela Rivers where the Ohio River was formed was a strategic link in the chain of French influence because water travel was critical to their mobility. England also claimed this area and was determined to occupy this point. An earlier attempt to expel the French from this location had ended with tragic consequences, but in 1757, it was time to move against this point again.

On May 30, 1757, Col. John Stanwix arrived outside the town of Carlisle with five companies of the Royal American 62nd Regiment and 250 men of Col. John Armstrong's battalion of provincial troops. They established a camp on the banks of the LeTort Spring Run to organize a base for operations against the French in western Pennsylvania. Through the following years this British post grew and became an important supply and manufacturing facility to support their operations. Eventually the French and their Native American allies were subdued and British control over western Pennsylvania was established. By the end of the French and Indian War, the Carlisle military post was a formidable supply depot employing many artisans and craftsmen. It was an ironic twist of fate that 20 years later this facility established to support British military operations would become a contributing factor in the expulsion of the British from the very colonies they had fought so hard to protect from the French and Native American threat.

When the American colonies rose up against British rule, their challenge was to build a system to supply and support their infant military establishment. It was a huge undertaking to take on one of the world's superpowers, and support for that effort would have to be extensive and consistent. The military facility at Carlisle came into American hands at the outset of the Revolution. Its facilities were untouched and it was soon put to use gathering supplies and livestock and manufacturing everything from uniforms and weapons to wagons, artillery, and ammunition. The U.S. Army's first schools were established at the facility to train its officers and soldiers. George Washington's Continental army was kept in the field largely because of the support it received from the Carlisle facility. In recognition of this the base was named Washingtonburg.

Following the Revolution, the US Army retained the facility for storage, recruiting, and training, and it continued in this capacity throughout the early 19th century. When the Civil War erupted, the post continued to support the northern war effort by providing training for regular army recruits and taking in supplies. In June 1863, the southern army invaded Pennsylvania and several alumni of Carlisle Barracks service returned for an awkward reunion. Elements of Gen. Robert E. Lee's army reached the area and occupied the town and the post before being ordered to concentrate in Adams County, just south of Carlisle, where the battle at Gettysburg would soon erupt. Gen. J. E. B. Stuart's cavalry arrived outside Carlisle on July 1 to find the town defended by U.S. forces. His demand for the surrender of the town was refused and Stuart responded by shelling the town with artillery and burning the barracks before being summoned to Gettysburg. After the southern occupation of the town and subsequent battle at Gettysburg, the barracks was rebuilt and its functions continued unchanged.

After the Civil War, the U.S. Army's Cavalry School continued to train soldiers at Carlisle until 1871 when the school was sent west to Jefferson Barracks, Missouri, and ultimately to Fort Riley, Kansas. With the departure of the Cavalry School the post was closed. In 1879, in another ironic twist of fate, Capt. Richard Pratt arrived with a mandate to establish a school to educate Native American children in the culture of the white man in an attempt to foster understanding between the two cultures. The Cavalry School had trained soldiers to fight the Native Americans on the western frontier, but after its departure, the Native Americans came to Carlisle to learn about the white man. The Carlisle Indian Industrial School flourished under Pratt's leadership for 25 years until his retirement in 1904. The school closed in 1918 due to the demands of World War I. With the requirement for hospital facilities because of the war, the U.S. Army reestablished its control of the post to organize a hospital facility there. This eventually led to the establishment of the U.S. Army's Medical Field Service School at Carlisle in 1920 to capture the lessons learned on the battlefields and to educate new army medical personnel. The Medical Field Service School remained at Carlisle until 1946 when it was moved to Fort Sam Houston, Texas.

Additional schools were operated at Carlisle Barracks until 1951 when they were relocated to other facilities and the U.S. Army War College was moved to the post from Fort Leavenworth, Kansas. Since that time the U.S. Army War College has been augmented by the Strategic Studies Institute, the army's Physical Fitness Institute, the Center for Strategic Leadership, and the U.S. Army Heritage and Education Center.

Col. John Stanwix could never have imagined the chain of events he set in motion on that May afternoon in 1757 when he established his camp along a creek in the Pennsylvania countryside. Carlisle Barracks has been a crossroads of history for over 250 years. The number of significant personalities who have walked its grounds is astounding. While an entire book could be written about them, that is not the purpose of this book. Carlisle Barracks is a stage upon which history has happened. The actors have come and gone and continue to do so, but the physical reality of that stage remains. It has changed over the years to meet the demands placed upon it, and this book is about that stage upon which history has occurred. Through the camera's eye we will examine the history and evolution of Carlisle Barracks and touch upon some of those personalities who have crossed that stage. The photographic images handed down to us will allow us to open a window in time to look back upon selected moments in the past that will serve as guideposts in our journey of examining this history. History is still being made at Carlisle Barracks, and educating and training our nation's military leaders is still the mission of this post. The story is still being written.

One

THE EARLY YEARS

The flag of Great Britain flew over Pennsylvania in the middle of the 18th century. Britain had great hopes for the North American colonies and the resources that lay inland from the Atlantic seaboard. (Author's collection.)

In 1730, settlers crossed the Susquehanna River to claim land. In 1750, Cumberland County was established, and the village of Carlisle was founded as the county seat in 1751. These settlements encroached upon lands given to the Native Americans and resulted in friction between the Native Americans and the British. As a result, many tribes began forming alliances with the French who were moving into western territories also claimed by the British. (Courtesy USAHEC.)

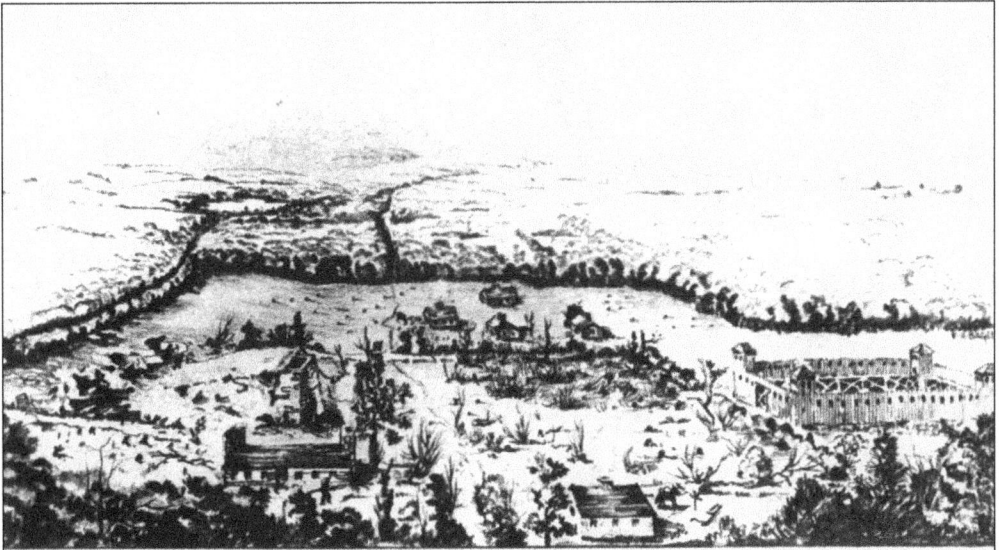

CARLISLE IN 1753

Native Americans began raiding the Cumberland Valley in the early 1750s. Carlisle was only a wide spot in the woods defended by a small stockade garrisoned by a group of provincial soldiers. As Native American depredations increased in the area, people took refuge at Carlisle seeking shelter and strength in numbers. (Courtesy USAHEC.)

War broke out between England and France. French forces in western Pennsylvania were centered at Fort Duquesne (now Pittsburgh) in territory claimed by Britain. In 1755, British general Edward Braddock, leading a force against the French at Fort Duquesne, was defeated on July 9 and was killed. His defeat placed great importance on Carlisle as a bulwark against French operations directed against eastern Pennsylvania. (Courtesy USAHEC.)

11

On May 30, 1757, Col. John Stanwix arrived at Carlisle with five companies of the Royal American 62nd Regiment and 250 men of Col. John Armstrong's battalion of provincial troops in preparation to move against the French. However, word was received that French forces were moving against central Pennsylvania, so Stanwix remained at Carlisle and constructed a fortified camp that would eventually become Carlisle Barracks. (Courtesy USAHEC.)

Stanwix's force camped along the LeTort Spring Run just east of Carlisle. The creek still runs through Carlisle Barracks, and parts of it probably look very much as it did to the British soldiers on that May afternoon in 1757. (Author's collection.)

Between 1757 and 1764, the post became a center of British activity to support operations against the French and Native Americans. Stanwix's successor, Gen. John Forbes, created a major supply depot, building barracks, storehouses, and manufacturing facilities. Col. Henry Bouquet trained British forces in counterguerilla tactics there in order to deal with the Native Americans. From here, Forbes captured Fort Duquesne in 1758, and Bouquet's troops defeated Chief Pontiac in 1763–1764. (Courtesy USAHEC.)

When British and American relations resulted in the Revolution in 1776, Carlisle Barracks supported Gen. George Washington's army. The facilities that had supported British soldiers were now turned to acquiring and producing everything Washington needed to keep his army in the field. The post was expanded to meet that need and from 1777 to the end of the Revolution almost every article used by the Continental forces was either manufactured or shipped from Carlisle. (Courtesy USAHEC.)

During the Revolution, the post was renamed Washingtonburg, and one of the buildings was a structure intended to serve as the commandant's quarters and post headquarters. This conjectural sketch shows the probable appearance of the first structure built to serve this purpose. Tradition says that it was built on the site of Col. John Stanwix's camp when he established the post and where his headquarters had been located. (Courtesy USAHEC.)

14

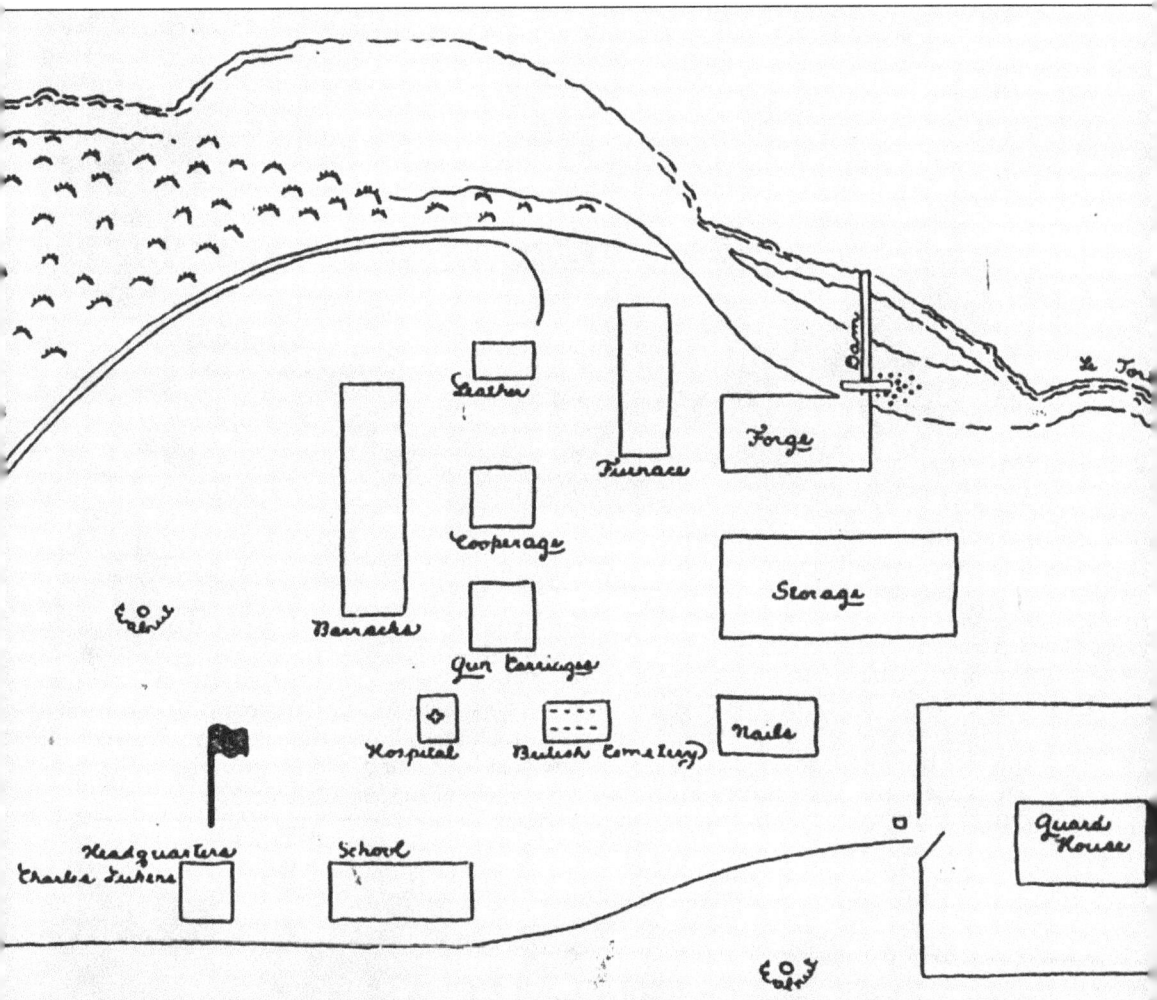

This map depicts the post during the time it was known as Washingtonburg. The various workshops are noted, and the one barracks is seen at left center. The headquarters building noted at lower left, with Maj. Charles Lukens as commandant, is the site of the post headquarters throughout much of the post's history. (Courtesy USAMHI.)

During this time, Hessian prisoners captured at the Battle of Trenton were sent to Carlisle to provide labor. One of the structures built during this expansion was a limestone powder magazine for the storage of powder produced at the post. Tradition indicates that Hessian prisoners built this structure although no direct documentation has been found. The magazine survives to this day as one of the oldest structures on Carlisle Barracks. (Courtesy USAMHI.)

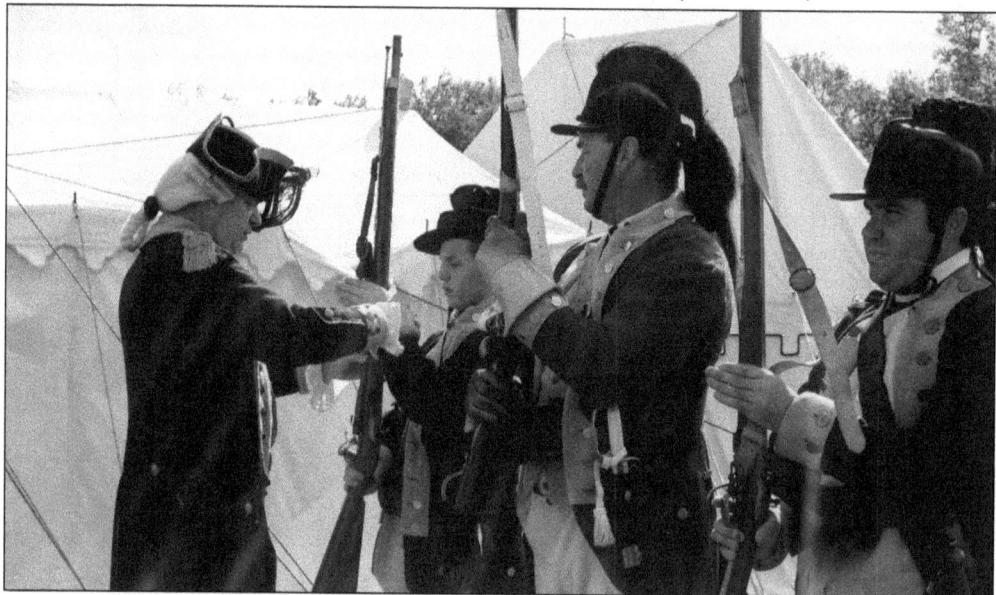

The end of the Revolutionary War in 1781 brought independence to the country, but it also brought downsizing to Carlisle Barracks as troops and artisans were relocated elsewhere. Excess material was sold off, and soon the facility was placed in a caretaker status. It was not until 1791 that the post was reopened as a base for recruit training and became a major storage facility for federally owned property. (Courtesy USAHEC.)

16

In 1794, the post was the camp for the army assembled by Pres. George Washington to quell what is known as the Whiskey Rebellion. This challenge to the government was caused by a dispute over taxation on whiskey. Farmers in western Pennsylvania found it easier to transport corn to market as whiskey rather than hauling the corn. Taxing whiskey and not corn was the problem, and they refused to pay the tax. (Courtesy USAHEC.)

Washington came to Carlisle, and on October 4, 1794, he reviewed the troops from the corner of High Street and West Street in Carlisle as they departed. In the end, the show of force convinced the rebellious farmers to back down. Although the whiskey tax was never collected, other taxes provided funds for the government. (Author's collection.)

This mill, built between 1761 and 1768, was operated as Wilson's Mill until 1810 when William Henderson acquired the property, and his family operated Henderson's Feed Mill until 1913. It provided feed and flour for Carlisle Barracks for many years. In 1926, the building was converted to apartments, and the U.S. Army acquired it on May 10, 1959, operating it as Mill Apartments for housing. It is the oldest building still standing on the post. (Author's collection.)

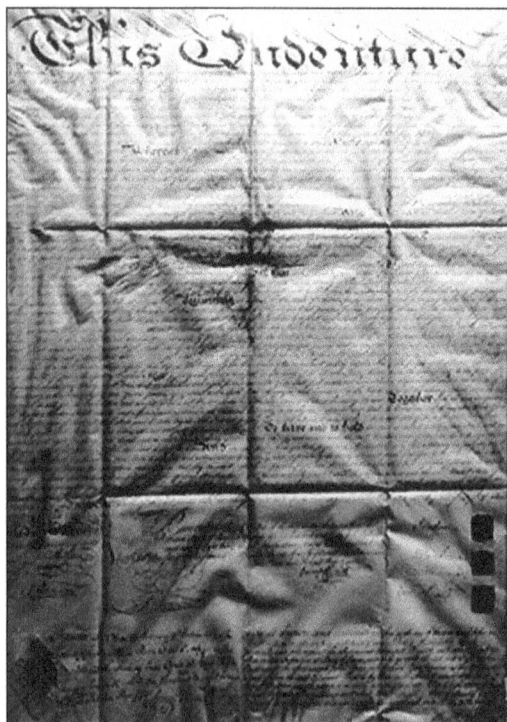

In 1801, the government purchased the post property from the heirs of William Penn for $664.20. Prior to that time, the property had been rented. The original deed is today part of the holdings of the U.S. Army Heritage and Education Center at Carlisle Barracks. In 1803, Lt. Col. Thomas Cushing provided eight recruits from Carlisle to assist Meriwether Lewis in preparation for his exploration of the Missouri River. (Courtesy USAHEC.)

In December 1806, a great fire destroyed many of the buildings on post, but with the onset of the War of 1812, the post was rebuilt and opened as a recruit depot to outfit and train over 100 men a week. By 1819, the post was placed into a caretaker status, and in 1828, the U.S. Navy was authorized to use the post as a recruiting depot. (Courtesy USAHEC.)

In 1838, the U.S. Army's Cavalry School was established at the post and an artillery school the next year. The post was the U.S. Army's training depot for cavalry, dragoons, and artillery. When the Mexican War broke out in 1846, the garrison deployed there, serving with distinction at the Battle of Buena Vista. With the end of that conflict, the post reverted to its function as a cavalry and artillery training center. (Courtesy USAHEC.)

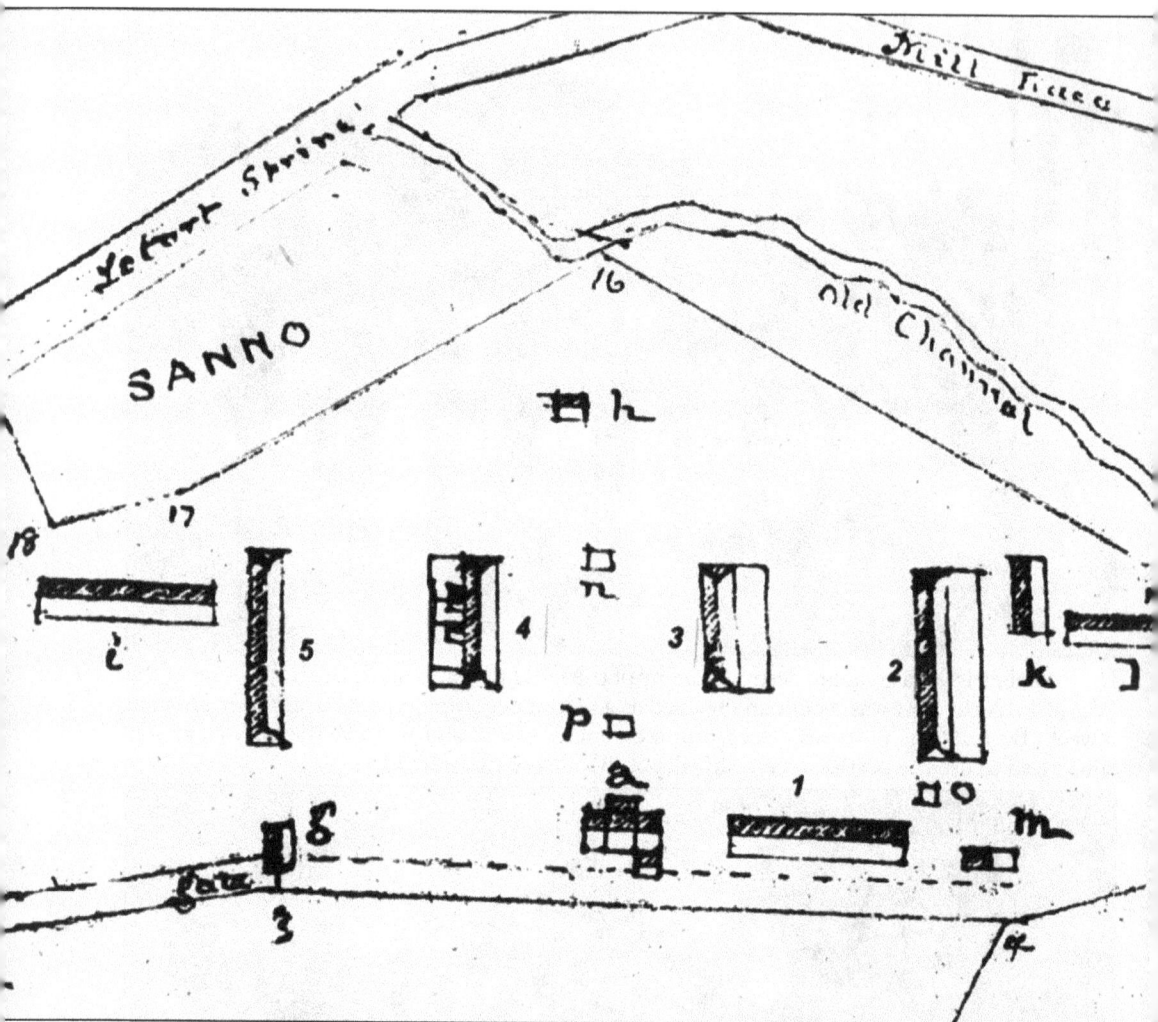

Between 1850 and 1860, there were several large fires on post necessitating construction of replacement structures. This map shows the post as it appeared in the early 19th century. Barracks 1 and 2 were soldier barracks. Barracks 3 and 4 were officers' quarters. Barracks 5 housed recruits. Barracks 3 sits on the site of the first noted barracks on the Washingtonburg map on page 15. Building a is the commandant's quarters and headquarters. Building g is the Hessian powder magazine, now serving as a guardhouse. (Courtesy USAMHI.)

Two

THE CIVIL WAR

In 1861, the nation found itself at war between North and South. Divided loyalties came between many U.S. Army officers serving at Carlisle Barracks. The firing on Fort Sumter sparked conflict, and Carlisle Barracks became a major supply and recruiting depot to support federal operations against the southern states. The post became a key facility for the recruiting and training of the U.S. Regular Cavalry. (Courtesy USAHEC.)

This map shows the post as it appeared in 1870 and represents what it looked like during the Civil War. Shown on the map are barracks 1, married soldiers; barracks 2, garrison soldiers and the band; barracks 3 and 4, officers' quarters; barracks 5, recruits; building 6, commandant's quarters; building 7, Hessian guardhouse; building 11, the stable; building 14, hospital; building 20, adjutant's quarters; building 21, sutler store; building 22, officers' stables; building 24, washhouses; and No. 26, cisterns. (Courtesy USAMHI.)

In April 1861, C. L. Lochman produced stereoscopic views of Carlisle Barracks. This scene shows guard mount with barracks 3 behind the formation. The adjutant presents the guard to the officer of the day, with his back to the camera. A cistern house is seen at far left center with one of the cannon houses to the left of it. See the illustration on page 34. (Courtesy USAMHI.)

Here is the site from the previous image as seen today. The barracks eventually burned in 1924, and a tennis court was constructed on its site. It is interesting to note that most of the sidewalks around the old parade ground still follow essentially the same routes as shown in photographs taken over a century ago. (Author's collection.)

This image is one of C. L. Lochman's stereoscopic views taken in April 1861. The view looks toward barracks 3 where a group of people is seen collected on the steps. To the right of the group is noted a large, leaning tree trunk. This tree is the key to identifying the location of the next image. The large tree trunks are whitewashed in order to make them more visible at night. (Courtesy USAMHI.)

This is the site from the previous photograph as seen today. The barracks is gone, replaced by a tennis court. (Author's collection.)

Here is another Lochman image with people visible in the view on the previous page. Barracks 3 is behind the group, and the tree trunk noted previously is to the right. Standing at center rear is the officer of the day, as evidenced by his sash. Seated at center is Capt. George Stoneman, who was at the post in April 1861. The man in white trousers on the ground is T. Scott Stewart, a horse buyer for the U.S. Army. (Courtesy USAMHI.)

Lochman turned his camera around and photographed the view back toward barracks 4 from where the top image on page 24 was taken. The two white-painted trees at center are also seen in this image on page 24. (Courtesy USAMHI.)

This is an artist's conjectural sketch of what the commandant's quarters looked like after 1849 when the two side wings were added to the structure. (Courtesy USAMHI.)

This is another C. L. Lochman image showing the commandant's quarters in April 1861. This photograph had been unidentified in the U.S. Army Military History Institute (USAMHI) holdings until this publication, and this may be the only pre–Civil War image of the structure. This was the structure that Fitz Lee's troopers burned in July 1863. Note the porch posts and horizontal strips, which relate to the next image. (Courtesy USAMHI.)

This C. L. Lochman image was taken on the front steps of the commandant's quarters. The three women standing are also present in the top image on page 25, as are the two soldiers standing and the soldier sitting on the stairs. Capt. George Stoneman is also seen here in civilian attire, sitting on the steps. Note the porch posts and horizontal strips as seen in the previous image that help identify this location. (Courtesy USAMHI.)

This image of a formation of cavalry troops at Carlisle Barracks is also one of Lochman's images taken in April 1861. It illustrates quite clearly what was one of the post's major functions as home to the Cavalry School, which was to train new cavalrymen. (Courtesy USAMHI.)

Quartering the number of horses needed to run the Cavalry School required extensive stables and support facilities. Out of frame to the far left was the blacksmith shop where horses were shod. The two identical buildings at center are actually a U-shaped building that was the primary stable facility. The building at right was the stable for the officers' horses. (Courtesy USAMHI.)

Carlisle Barracks received recruits and trained cavalrymen and artillerymen. Because many recruits were drawn to the attractions of nearby Carlisle and were often AWOL, an eight-foot-high plank fence was constructed around the entire post. Although only a slight obstacle to those who were determined to go over it, the fence became a Carlisle Barracks fixture for many years. (Courtesy USAHEC.)

The war raged only a short distance south of Pennsylvania, and while there was concern about southern incursions into the Carlisle area, it did not appear likely the war would intrude that far north. However, in June 1863, Gen. Robert E. Lee's Confederate army moved into Maryland and Pennsylvania, advancing up the Cumberland Valley heading toward Harrisburg. (Courtesy USAHEC.)

In the face of advancing Confederate forces, Carlisle Barracks was evacuated on June 25, 1863, with supplies and recruits sent to Harrisburg. At 11:00 a.m. on June 27, the advance of Gen. Richard Ewell's corps arrived in Carlisle when Gen. Albert G. Jenkins arrived with 400 cavalrymen. He told the city fathers to provide 1,500 rations to be gathered at the market house. Ewell's troops soon followed. (Courtesy Library of Congress.)

Gen. Richard Ewell's corps entered Carlisle at 5:00 p.m., camping in the community and occupying Carlisle Barracks where Ewell established his headquarters. In 1840, Ewell had served at the barracks and knew the post and community very well. Many Confederates had either served at the barracks or been students at Dickinson College and took the opportunity to call on friends and acquaintances in the community. (Courtesy Library of Congress.)

Ewell, his staff, and elements of his corps entered Carlisle Barracks through the gate adjacent to the old Hessian powder magazine guardhouse. They occupied the post, and Ewell established his headquarters here for operations against Harrisburg. The plank fence constructed around the post is clearly visible here, as is the city of Carlisle to the right distance, beyond the Hessian guardhouse. (Courtesy USAMHI.)

The Confederates foraged supplies and sent elements to Mechanicsburg where they skirmished with U.S. forces near Harrisburg. On June 29, Ewell received orders to rejoin Robert E. Lee's army at Gettysburg, and on that day and the next his forces left Carlisle. With the removal of federal and Confederate forces, many citizens visited Carlisle Barracks, where they plundered the post and destroyed a great deal of property. (Courtesy USAHEC.)

On July 1, Capt. William H. Boyd of the 1st New York Cavalry arrived in Carlisle, followed later by Gen. William F. "Baldy" Smith in command of the federal forces in the Cumberland Valley. He was accompanied by three Pennsylvania militia regiments, the 28th, 30th, and 33rd, the 22nd and 37th New York National Guard regiments, and a battery of artillery. The contingent numbered about 3,000 men. (Courtesy USAHEC.)

Gen. J. E. B. Stuart's Confederate cavalry, numbering about 3,500 men, arrived outside Carlisle about 6:30 p.m. on July 1, expecting to meet Confederate forces there, but Gen. Richard Ewell had departed the previous day, and Gen. William F. Smith's division was in possession of the town. When Smith refused Stuart's demand to surrender the town, Stuart threatened to shell it. (Courtesy Library of Congress.)

The city's defenders had prepared defenses by barricading High Street and other avenues of approach. Many large shade trees along the city's streets were sacrificed to form a barricade against a mounted cavalry charge. This view looks down High Street toward the Confederate positions and shows one of these barricades in the upper left distance. A section of artillery was placed in the street. (Courtesy of Harper's Weekly.)

Another demand for the city's surrender was refused, and Stuart opened fire on the city, expending 134 rounds of ammunition. About 9:30 p.m., Stuart ordered Brig. Gen. Fitz Lee to send his cavalry troopers to burn Carlisle Barracks and the nearby city gasworks. Sparks from these fires also ignited a lumberyard, and by 11:00 p.m., great sheets of fire were spread across the northeastern horizon. (Courtesy USAMHI.)

Brig. Gen. Fitz Lee had a bittersweet reunion since he had served at Carlisle Barracks after graduating from West Point, taught horsemanship at the Cavalry School, and became known in the community. On this night, his orders were to destroy something that was a pleasant memory to him. Overnight, Stuart learned that Lee was engaged in battle 25 miles to the south at Gettysburg, so Stuart's troops departed at 3:00 a.m. on July 2 to rejoin the Confederates. (Courtesy Library of Congress.)

The Cumberland County Courthouse had provided one of many targets for Gen. J. E. B. Stuart's artillery, and even today, evidence of the bombardment can be seen around Carlisle. One of the most visible scars can be found on one of the columns of the county courthouse. (Author's collection.)

On July 2, 1863, Gen. William F. Smith moved his headquarters to Carlisle Barracks. Only the burned-out shells of its structures remained. However, the adjutant's quarters were untouched, and Smith established his headquarters there. This period sketch shows the burned-out ruins of barracks 2 in the rear and barracks 3 at left. Visible next to the wagon in the center background is a cistern house, and the plank fence around the post is visible beyond that. (Courtesy USAMHI.)

34

The same view today shows the tennis court that occupies the site of barracks 3 and Upton Hall in the center distance that occupies the site of barracks 2. (Author's collection.)

Smith's troops remained at the barracks until July 4, when they departed. This image is another part of the period sketch noted previously and shows the ruins of barracks 1. It is interesting to note that this sketch shows barracks 1 as a three-story structure although when it was reconstructed it was built as a two-story structure. (Courtesy USAMHI.)

This is the same view today. The adjutant's quarters are gone, having once stood in the space to the left of the commandant's quarters. Today officers' quarters stand where barracks 1 once stood. (Author's collection.)

The adjutant's quarters were not burned. The building had been the home of Michael Sanno, a War of 1812 veteran who had been employed at the post for many years. He had become a favorite of many of the soldiers who served at the post, to include Fitz Lee. When Lee issued orders for the destruction of the post, he also issued an order to spare the home of "old Pop Sanno," and this was done. (Courtesy USAMHI.)

An assessment revealed that the buildings could be rebuilt at a cost of $47,600, and the work was underway by October 1863. Garrison troops moved into tents and hut encampments while functions were reestablished in temporary structures. The post continued to support the U.S. Army until the end of the war. This image taken by D. C. Burnite of Harrisburg in 1867 shows the reconstructed commandant's quarters. (Courtesy USAMHI.)

The same view today shows the old commandant's quarters, reflecting the changes made in 1913. (Author's collection.)

Another image by D. C. Burnite taken in 1867 shows reconstructed barracks 2 with garrison soldiers lounging outside. The white line running off through the grass at right marks the drain from this barracks where rainwater was directed to a cistern located out of picture to the right. This cistern is depicted in the sketch of the burned post on page 34 and is also visible in the photograph of the Indian School hospital on page 67. (Courtesy USAMHI.)

Upton Hall occupies the site of barracks 2 today. (Author's collection.)

A detailed image drawn from the photograph on the previous page shows the soldiers relaxing outside barracks 2. In this age without electricity, the Internet, television, cell phones, and such, the soldiers had to find other forms of diversion when they had time on their hands. The three young boys in the foreground are probably dependents. (Courtesy USAMHI.)

Another detail view drawn from the top image on page 38 shows soldiers relaxing outside barracks 2. Some are reading newspapers while others sit in the shade. Many of these men are probably Civil War veterans. (Courtesy USAMHI.)

Another image taken by D. C. Burnite of Harrisburg shows barracks 3 to the right and barracks 4 to the left. The four cannon houses noted on the map on page 22 can be discerned at center. In the distant center is a group of soldiers gathered who appear to be engaged in constructing the bandstand that was built in 1867, which dates this series of images. (Courtesy USAMHI.)

This is the same view today. Only barracks 4 remains, and the bandstand has been replaced. (Author's collection.)

A detail of the previous image of barracks 3 shows the white-painted trees seen in the views on pages 24 and 25 and the site of the image on page 25 taken by the large tree at right center. (Courtesy USAMHI.)

In this enlargement from the top view on page 40, the soldiers appears to be working on installing the foundation for the bandstand. In the background can be seen two of the four cannon houses noted as located here. A 12-pound Napoleon field piece was stored in each house, probably for drill purposes. (Courtesy USAMHI.)

Another detail image drawn from the top view on page 40 shows barracks 4 with the foliage of springtime in full bloom. (Courtesy USAMHI.)

Here is another image of barracks 4, but now it is seen in the dead of winter, probably dating to the post-1868 period. See the image on the top of page 62 for the same scene 20 years later. (Courtesy USAMHI.)

This is another 1867 D. C. Burnite image of the parade ground that looks back in the opposite direction from the previous views. Barracks 3 is seen at right, barracks 4 is beyond that at center, and barracks 5 is in the distance beyond the flagpole. At left are dependent children watching the troops drill. (Courtesy USAMHI.)

Here is the same view as seen today. (Author's collection.)

This detail image shows barracks 5 in the background and a group of cavalrymen in formation being observed by the children in the foreground. The immense size of the flagpole is clearly evident here when compared to the size of the soldiers adjacent to it. (Courtesy USAMHI.)

This is another detail image showing the cavalrymen formed up along the sidewalk with the end of barracks 4 beyond. (Courtesy USAMHI.)

Here is a detail image of the cavalrymen drawn up along the sidewalk. The wooden foundation of the bandstand can be seen behind them. (Courtesy USAMHI.)

The line of cavalrymen seen in the previous image extends along the parade ground beside barracks 3. The small tree growing up beside the barracks will become an important reference point in identifying the photograph location of Sioux girls on page 54. (Courtesy USAMHI.)

This photograph by D. C. Burnite shows post commandant Gen. John P. Hatch posing with a group following a croquet game, evidenced by the balls and mallets on the ground at lower right. Barracks 3 is in the background. A cistern is seen behind the Napoleon gun at left as a flat, circular spot on the ground. The cannons represent three of the four guns housed in the cannon houses noted on the 1870 map and located out of frame to the left. (Courtesy USAMHI.)

Here is the same view as seen today. The trees still provide a shady spot; however, barracks 3 is gone, replaced by a tennis court. (Author's collection.)

46

A detailed view from the previous page shows a group of lieutenants playing cards with a female companion. Clearly seen behind the artillery piece is the circular cover over the cistern. (Courtesy USAMHI.)

The officer of the day is seen seated at center with sword and sash. Family members sit at right while a young boy reclines at left. People sitting on the steps of barracks 3 can be seen in the distant left background. (Courtesy USAMHI.)

Gen. John P. Hatch, post commandant, sits at right with a croquet mallet on his lap. Hatch saw considerable service during the Civil War and served as post commandant from 1868 to 1870. (Courtesy USAMHI.)

With trouble out west with hostile Native Americans, the Cavalry School was closed on April 20, 1871, and moved to Jefferson Barracks at St. Louis and eventually to Fort Riley, Kansas. In July 1871, Carlisle Barracks was closed and placed in a caretaker status. (Courtesy USAMHI.)

The commandant's quarters are pictured as seen on a cold winter day after the Cavalry School had been closed. (Courtesy USAMHI.)

Here is the same view as seen today. (Author's collection.)

The parade ground, where British soldiers had marched, where the U.S. Cavalry had drilled, and where Confederate soldiers had torched the post, was quiet. In 1871, its future was uncertain. For several years, the post remained quiet until 1879 when an ironic turn of events took place. (Courtesy USAMHI.)

Here is the same view as seen today, 140 years later. (Author's collection.)

Three

THE INDIAN
INDUSTRIAL SCHOOL

After Carlisle Barracks closed in 1871, it remained in a caretaker status while ideas were explored as to how the post might be used. In 1878, General-in-Chief William T. Sherman recommended the post be sold, since he felt the U.S. Army would have no further use for the facility. But there were others who felt the post would be an ideal place for a revolutionary idea in education. (Courtesy USAMHI.)

Capt. Richard Pratt had advocated for the education of Native American youth in the culture and professions of white society. Early attempts had shown promise, but Pratt desired a facility dedicated to Native American education. Carlisle Barracks offered that facility, and an effort was made to acquire it. The U.S. Army transferred the post to the Department of the Interior in September 1879, and the Carlisle Indian Industrial School, referred to often as just the Indian School, was established. (Courtesy USAMHI.)

The plan was to convince selected Native American chiefs to allow their children to be sent from their reservations to Carlisle where they would be educated in white culture and taught skills and vocations that would allow them to survive in a changing world. Here Yellow Bear, an Arapahoe chief, poses with his daughter Minnie. One can imagine the sense of culture shock experienced by many of these Native American children. (Courtesy USAMHI.)

The first group of 37 Sioux Indian boys arrived at the school on October 6, 1879. They had traveled from the Rosebud and Pine Ridge Sioux agencies in Dakota and are posed here in front of barracks 2, which would be used as the large boys' dormitory. Pratt is standing at left, and interpreter Charles Tackett is standing at right. The school opened on November 1, 1879, with 147 students. (Courtesy USAMHI.)

Upton Hall now occupies the site of barracks 2, and there is little to indicate what occurred here in that moment of time in 1879. (Author's collection.)

The first group of 25 Sioux girls from the Rosebud and Pine Ridge Sioux agencies also arrived at the school on October 6, 1879. They are posed here at the end of barracks 3, which would be used as the girls' dormitory. S. A. Mather, their chaperone, stands at left, and interpreter Charles Tackett stands at right. Note the tree behind them, which locates this scene and is noted in the images of barracks 3 on pages 45 and 61. (Courtesy USAMHI.)

The same view today shows the tennis court that occupies the former site of barracks 3. (Author's collection.)

Within months, the school had immersed the Native American children in the culture and ways of white America. Here is a group of Chiricahua Apaches seen as they arrived at the Indian School on November 4, 1886. (Courtesy USAMHI.)

Here are the same Chiricahua Apache children from the previous photograph seen four months after their arrival at the school. The boys wear the standard military-style uniform prescribed for male students, and the girls wear appropriately styled dresses for female students. (Courtesy USAMHI.)

Pueblo Indians pose in their traditional dress. (Courtesy USAMHI.)

The trio of Pueblo Indians from the previous image is shown here in Indian School uniforms. They are identified by their anglicized names, from left to right, Sheldon Jackson, Harvey Townsend, and John Shields. (Courtesy USAMHI.)

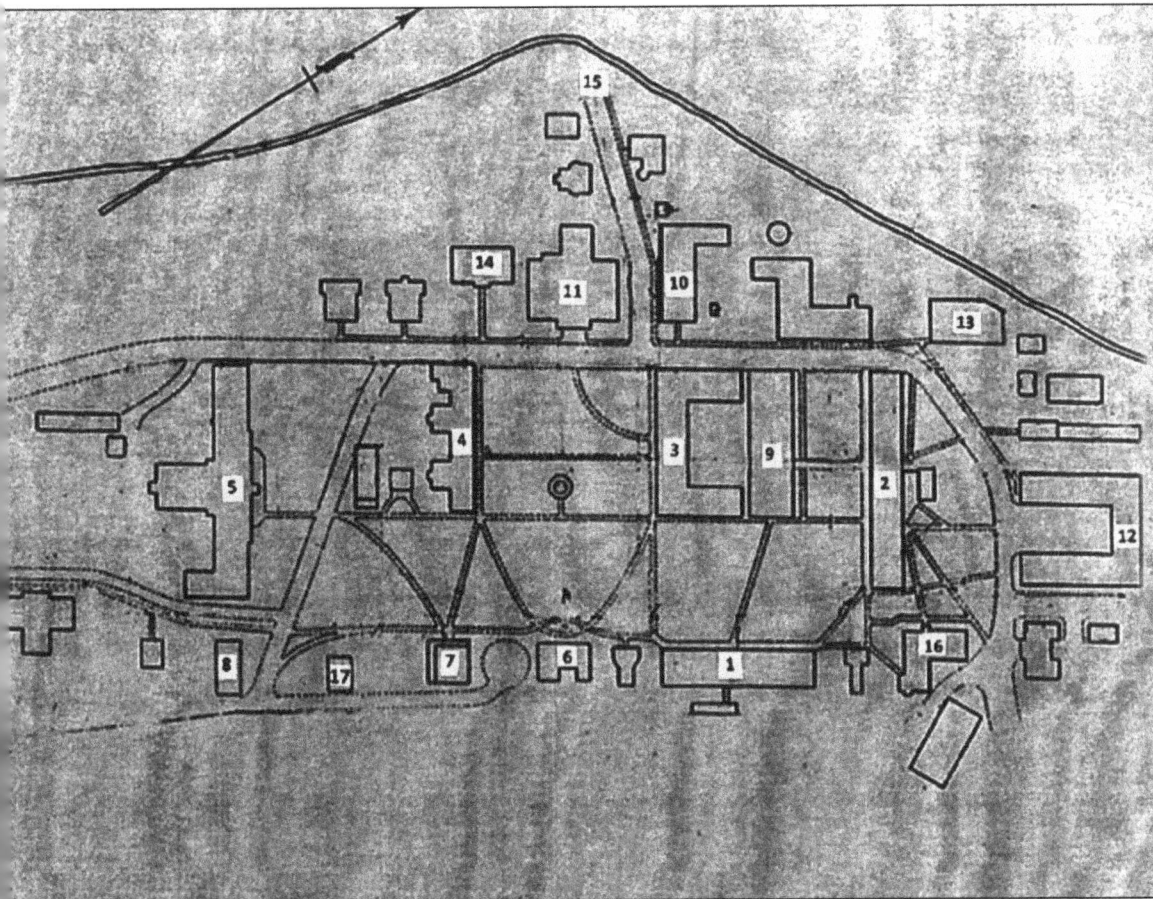

The old post went through an ongoing adaptation of buildings and construction of new facilities. This map shows the layout of the post during the Indian School. Shown on the map are barracks 1, the small boys' dormitory (1); barracks 2, the large boys' dormitory (2); barracks 3, the girls' dormitory (3); barracks 4, teachers' quarters (4); barracks 5, academic building (5); superintendent's quarters (6); administration office (7); Hessian guardhouse (8); gymnasium (9); laundry (10); dining facility (11); industrial building (12); commissary (13); print shop (14); entrance (15); hospital then athletes' dormitory (16); and chapel (17). (Author's collection.)

This group image shows the students of the school drawn up on the parade ground. Behind them are, from right to left, the superintendent's quarters, the adjutant's quarters, barracks 1 (small boys' dormitory), the old sutler store, and the hospital. See the image of the burned post on page 35. (Courtesy USAMHI.)

This group of Native American boys poses in front of barracks 1, the small boys' dormitory, in September 1894. Some wear their school uniforms while others are in civilian dress. (Courtesy USAMHI.)

Here is a full image of barracks 2, the large boys' dormitory, showing the boys drawn up wearing their school uniforms. The two small trees in this photograph and on page 53 show that the image on page 53 was posed in front of these trees. This barracks is also seen on page 38 but with soldiers lounging out front and on page 85. (Courtesy USAMHI.)

This is the same view today. The fire hydrant at right appears to be in the same location as the one seen in the previous image. (Author's collection.)

A detail image drawn from the previous page shows a group of Native American boys posed in front of barracks 2. (Courtesy USAMHI.)

Another detail image shows a group of Native American boys with a small child who is probably the daughter of one of the instructors. (Courtesy USAMHI.)

Pictured here is barracks 3, the girls' dormitory, with Native American girls posed out front. The bare trees indicate this to be winter, and the girls appear to be wrapped up with coats and blankets. The image of the first group of girls at the school was taken at the end of the building to the right where the tree is located. This tree is visible behind the group of girls in that image on page 54. See also the image on the top of page 86. (Courtesy USAMHI.)

Here is the same view as seen today. (Author's collection.)

This image of barracks 4 by John N. Choate of Carlisle shows the building shortly after the opening of the Indian School when the structure was being used as teachers' quarters. Capt. Richard Pratt's office was also located on the ground floor behind the two men standing on the porch. Pratt is seen standing at right facing his deputy superintendent Alfred Standing. (Courtesy USAMHI.)

This image shows the same view as seen today. Barracks 4 is the only surviving barracks. (Author's collection.)

A detailed view drawn from the previous page shows Pratt at right and Standing at left. (Courtesy USAMHI.)

Barracks 5, the old recruit barracks, stood empty for several years after the post was closed. When the Indian School was established, the barracks was converted to serve as classrooms. (Courtesy USAMHI.)

Another John N. Choate image shows barracks 5 after it was converted from a recruit barracks to an academic building for educational classes. Here the students are lining up prior to entering their respective classrooms. (Courtesy USAMHI.)

This is the same view as seen today. Barracks 5 survived until the late 1930s, when it was taken down. (Author's collection.)

A detail view drawn from the previous page shows Native American students lining up for their classes and awaiting the call to enter. (Courtesy USAMHI.)

Teachers greet their students at the classroom door. The small child seen sitting on the railing may be the same child seen in the bottom image on page 60. (Courtesy USAMHI.)

In 1889, barracks 5 was changed by having its center altered by the construction of a large addition as seen here. It contained offices, an auditorium, and classrooms. Eventually the two remaining wings of the original barracks were extended by additions constructed for that purpose. (Courtesy USAMHI.)

This view of barracks 5, now known as the academic building, shows the extended wing that resulted from the additions placed on the end of each wing of the building. (Courtesy USAMHI.)

A view across the parade ground shows the bandstand built 20 years prior, with barracks 4 and barracks 5 beyond. (Courtesy USAMHI.)

In 1884, a new hospital was constructed, which is shown here on the left. The building at right had been the sutler's store when the U.S. Army occupied the post. Original identification with this image indicates that this building was the "Disciplinarian's Quarters." At lower left in front of the hospital is a flat platform with a vertical projection. This is one of the two cisterns that collected rainwater from barracks runoff. It can be seen in the sketch on the bottom of page 34. (Courtesy USAMHI.)

The dining facility was constructed by Native American students in vocational training classes. The school used this method to train students and allowed them to enhance school facilities. Products made in vocational classes were sold and generated funds to undertake projects such as this dining facility. This structure served the Indian School, General Hospital No. 31, and the Medical Field Service School until 1922 when a fire in the kitchen destroyed the building. (Courtesy USAMHI.)

Pictured here is an interior view of the dining facility as it appeared decorated for Christmas. (Courtesy USAMHI.)

This is the same view as previously seen, except that now the students have taken their seats at the tables and await the holiday meal. (Courtesy USAMHI.)

The school taught numerous trades and occupations. The blacksmith shop once used to keep the horses shod at the Cavalry School now taught Native American students the skills of a trained blacksmith. This building stood near the LeTort Spring Run where Root Hall now stands. Please also see pages 73 and 113. (Courtesy USAMHI.)

Music was one of the many subjects that Native American students were exposed to. Here the school band poses on the bandstand. (Courtesy USAMHI.)

The success of the school necessitated an expansion of facilities. Buildings were refurbished or reconstructed mostly with funds raised by the Native American students. The girls' dormitory, seen here in 1884, was a two-story building when the school was established and enlarged by the addition of a third story and additional wings in the rear. The large boys' dormitory was also rebuilt and enlarged from a two-story building to a three-story building. (Courtesy USAMHI.)

70

Here the school band poses by the bandstand with the expanded girls' dormitory (barracks 3) seen behind it. (Courtesy USAMHI.)

Athletics was another area of instruction, and Glen S. "Pop" Warner fielded some of the best athletic teams in the nation. In 1887, students built a new gymnasium between barracks 2 and barracks 3, eventually named Thorpe Hall in honor of Jim Thorpe, who attended the school from 1904 to 1909 and 1911 to 1913. His fame as an athlete and his performance in the 1912 Olympics in Sweden brought national recognition to the school. (Courtesy USAMHI.)

Capt. Richard Pratt and his family lived in the old commandant's quarters during the time he operated the school. It was essentially the structure that had been rebuilt following the destruction of the post during the Civil War. (Courtesy USAMHI.)

In a detail view drawn from the previous image, Pratt can be seen standing in front of the building with his wife and young daughter while a visiting Native American chief stands to the right. (Courtesy USAMHI.)

1 312

In 1891, the Indian School students built this structure adjacent to the commandant's quarters to serve as the school's administrative offices. Built as a vocational project by Native American students with local contractor Andrew Wetzel, this building is again an example of the school's ability to raise funds, train students, and use the two for positive improvement of the facilities on the post. (Courtesy USAMHI.)

These buildings were part of the old cavalry presence on the post that the school put to use for its purposes. The blacksmith shop where Native American students learned that trade is just out of frame to the left. Please also see pages 69 and 113. The U-shaped building at center had been a stable from its cavalry days; however, the students converted it into workshops and industrial classrooms where these trades were taught. (Courtesy USAMHI.)

As the need for classroom space grew with the influx of new students, the old stables were enlarged by the addition of a second story thanks to a congressional appropriation for that purpose. (Courtesy USAMHI.)

This building was constructed by the students to serve as the printing shop where the printing trade was taught and where the school's publishing requirements were met. Over the years, it was enlarged and eventually became the officers' club. Today it serves as the post community center, and although hardly recognizable as the same building, the building seen here still stands and is still used. See page 115 for an additional view. (Courtesy USAMHI.)

The old Hessian powder magazine had ceased to serve that function and been converted to a guardhouse by the U.S. Army. The Indian School operated a student court composed of student representatives who adjudicated judicial actions against Native American students charged with infractions of the school's rules. When necessary, Native American students were confined here. (Courtesy USAMHI.)

When the expansion of the school required a new hospital, this structure was built, and the old hospital was converted to a dormitory facility for the school's athletic teams. (Courtesy USAMHI.)

In June 1894, Carlisle photographer John Leslie photographed the Native American students at play on the parade ground from the second-story porch of barracks 2, the large boys' dormitory. Barracks 5, the academic building, can be seen at distant right, and the Hessian guardhouse is seen at distant left. In the background between these two buildings, one can make out the plank fence that surrounded the post. (Courtesy USAMHI.)

Although barracks 2 is gone, Upton Hall sits on the same site and allows this comparison view from almost the exact vantage point as the boys' dormitory. (Author's collection.)

The Indian School Fire Department, composed of students, was another practical training exercise. Students not only learned about this profession but also provided protection against fires breaking out on post. Here they conduct a practice drill in the street in front of barracks 3, the girls' dormitory, much to the delight of the girls gathered to watch. (Courtesy USAMHI.)

Each year, a class of students graduated from the school, and Capt. Richard Pratt invited distinguished people to give the commencement address. The commencement of 1896 was an interesting one, since the speaker was Fitz Lee, whose forces had burned the post in July 1863. Lee's presence stirred up controversy in the community, but his visit was well received and evidence of the national reconciliation taking place at that time. (Courtesy USAMHI.)

In addition to Fitz Lee, Capt. Richard Pratt invited Maj. Gen. Oliver O. Howard, who also had a significant career during the Civil War and whose forces were engaged against the Confederate forces at Gettysburg that same July. To round out the list of invitees was Gov. D. H. Hastings of Pennsylvania, who was the son of the man that commanded Carlisle Barracks at the time that Lee's forces burned it. (Courtesy Library of Congress.)

In May 1904, Pratt (pictured) was relieved as superintendent of the school by Indian Bureau officials who disagreed with some of his plans for the school. He was replaced by Capt. (Major) William A. Mercer of the 7th Cavalry, who was replaced in 1908 by Moses Friedman. Friedman was succeeded in September 1914 by Dr. Oscar Lipps, an Indian agent. On April 18, 1917, Lt. John Francis Jr. superseded Lipps as the U.S. Army began to resume control of the post. (Courtesy USAMHI.)

The old commandant's quarters were substantially refurbished in 1913 during a period of overall campus reconditioning conducted by then superintendent Friedman. (Courtesy USAMHI.)

World War I contributed to the closing of the Indian School. Its usefulness had been debated, and the question was what to do about the future of the institution. In 1918, the U.S. Army reassumed control of the post in order to provide hospital facilities for wounded soldiers. The school existed for 39 years and was closed on September 1, 1918. (Courtesy USAHEC.)

Capt. Richard Pratt put his heart and soul into the school and was looked upon by the Native American students with great affection. Here the student body of the school poses in front of the commandant's quarters. The legacy of the Indian School can be seen today in the form of structures, the athletic field, and the poignant cemetery of the Native American students who passed away while at the school. (Courtesy USAMHI.)

The previous photograph was taken from the bandstand. This view shows the modern comparison image today. (Author's collection.)

Four

GENERAL HOSPITAL NO. 31 AND THE MEDICAL FIELD SERVICE SCHOOL

The U.S. Army reoccupied Carlisle Barracks in September 1918 and established General Hospital No. 31 as a rehabilitation center for the treatment of soldiers injured during America's involvement in World War I. The old buildings of the Indian School were converted to hospital functions. Most had been built in 1864, while others had been remodeled or constructed by the Indian School. Once again, the U.S. Army walked the historic parade ground. (Courtesy USAMHI.)

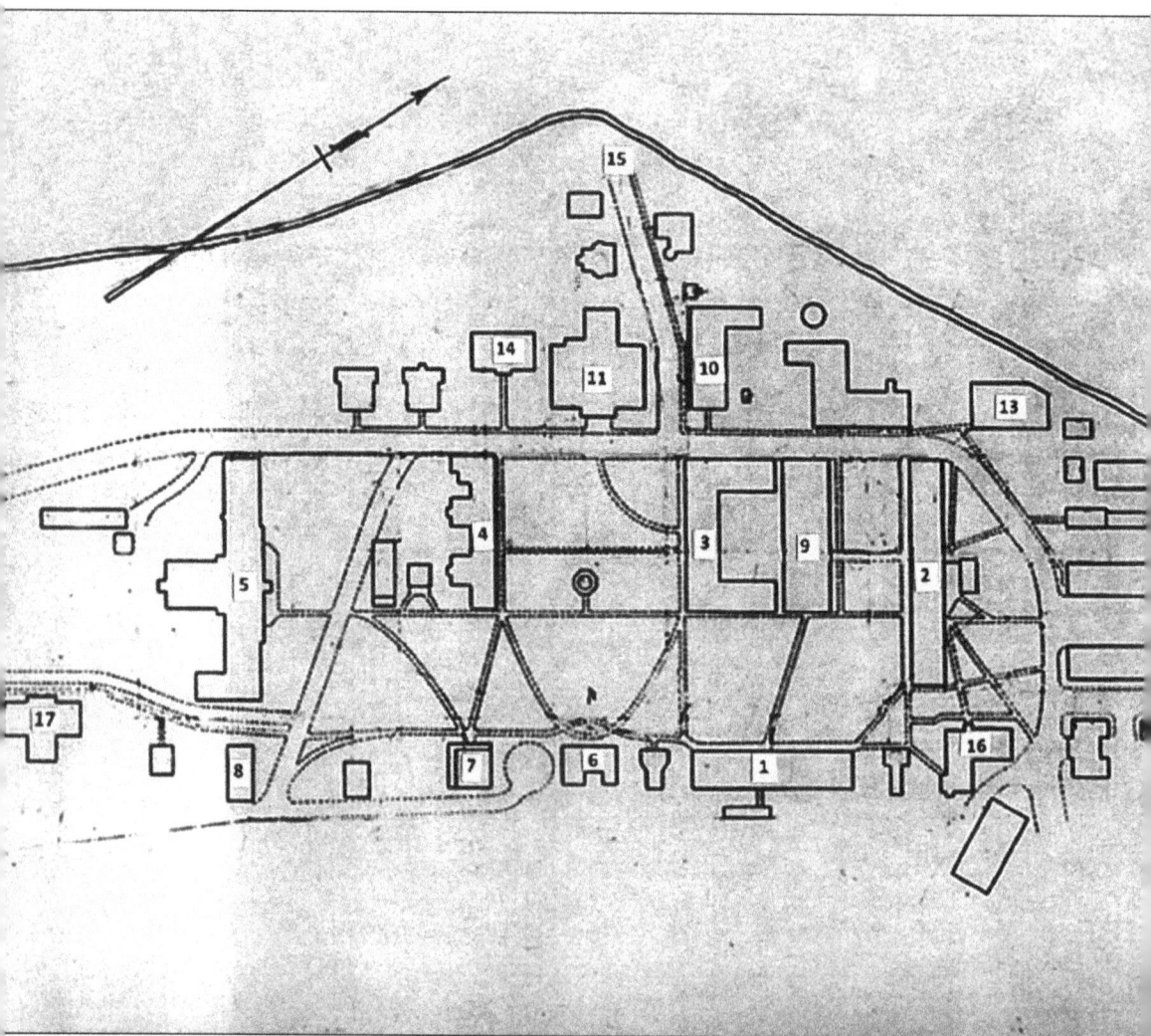

This map of the post depicts its appearance during the period of General Hospital No. 31 and the subsequent Medical Field Service School. Seen on the map are barracks 1, enlisted quarters (1); barracks 2, enlisted quarters (General Hospital No. 31), and academic building (Hoff Hall, school) (2); barracks 3, hospital wards (General Hospital No. 31), and student housing (school) (3); barracks 4, nurses' quarters (General Hospital No. 31), and officers' quarters (school) (4); barracks 5, hospital wards (General Hospital No. 31), and academic building (school) (5); commandant's quarters and officers' quarters (6); headquarters (7); Hessian guardhouse (8); gymnasium (9); Armstrong Hall and laundry (10); dining facility (11); classrooms (12); commissary (13); club (14); Pratt Avenue entrance (15); guesthouse and officers' quarters (16); and Pratt Hall and doctors' quarters (17). (Author's collection.)

The first patients arrived in December 1918, and the hospital functioned until September 1, 1920, when it closed after treating over 4,000 soldiers. Following the closure of the hospital, the Medical Field Service School was established at Carlisle Barracks using the lessons learned from World War I to develop doctrine and train medical service personnel. The first class arrived in May 1921. (Courtesy USAMHI.)

The parade ground was essentially the same as when the Cavalry School operated at the post. The Indian School had brought about some changes in structures and facilities such as the administration building seen at left center that would serve as the post headquarters and enlarged barracks, such as barracks 5. (Courtesy USAMHI.)

The old commandant's quarters where Capt. Richard Pratt had resided as superintendent of the Indian School became officers' quarters during the time that General Hospital No. 31 was in operation and continued to serve that function when the Medical Field Service School opened at the post. (Courtesy USAMHI.)

The administration building constructed by the Native American students served as post headquarters for both the hospital and the medical school. (Courtesy USAMHI.)

Barracks 1 served as enlisted quarters after serving many years as the small boys' dormitory during the Indian School period. (Courtesy USAMHI.)

Barracks 2, which had been the large boys' dormitory, served as hospital wards for wounded soldiers during the time General Hospital No. 31 operated on post. It then served as enlisted men's quarters during the early part of the medical school period until being turned over to academic use and named Hoff Hall in honor of Maj. John R. Hoff. Note the tree at center, a silent witness to the prior history that had occurred there. See this tree in the images on pages 53 and 59. (Courtesy USAMHI.)

Barracks 3, which had served as the girls' dormitory and been greatly expanded during the Indian School period, now housed Ward No. 20 during the hospital period. When the medical school opened, it was used as student housing. Compare this image to the one on page 61. (Courtesy USAMHI.)

Barracks 4 housed nurses during the hospital period and was then used as faculty and officers' quarters during the medical school period. This view was taken from the upper porch of the old commandant's quarters. (Courtesy USAMHI.)

Here is a view from the upper portico of the commandant's quarters that shows barracks 3 on the right, the bandstand at the left, and the dining facility beyond during the time that General Hospital No. 31 operated at the post. (Courtesy USAMHI.)

Barracks 5 served as the home of the 1st Medical Regiment and part of the station detachment during the hospital period and housed hospital wards and medical supply facilities. The auditorium built into the center by the Indian School was used as an assembly area and contained operating rooms. This building was eventually condemned in 1932, leading to the construction of Young Hall in 1936, which can be seen on the bottom of page 97. (Courtesy USAMHI.)

The Pratt Avenue entrance gave access to Hanover Street north of the post. The old traditional entrance at the Hessian guardhouse also continued to operate. Here vehicles are seen leaving the post in 1918. (Courtesy USAMHI.)

ENTRANCE DRIVE. U. S. ARMY GENERAL HOSPITAL No. 31. CARLISLE. PA.

Traffic is seen entering the post through the Pratt Avenue gate. The building on the right had been built as an art studio by the Indian School, but during the occupation of the post by General Hospital No. 31, it was utilized by the Red Cross. (Courtesy USAMHI.)

Armstrong Hall had served as the school laundry for the Indian School and for the U.S. Army when they reoccupied the post. To the left in this image is seen an electric trolley that provided transportation to and from Carlisle for soldiers at the post. It entered the post through the Pratt Avenue gate and could be boarded at Armstrong Hall for the short trip to Carlisle. (Courtesy USAMHI.)

The Pratt Avenue gate, as seen in winter with a solitary soldier walking guard, is a testament to the pre-9/11 perception of security. (Courtesy USAMHI.)

The Pratt Avenue gate still exists, but it no longer serves as an access point to the post. Today traffic passing here is generally looking for parking spaces to the left or the department of public works facilities to the right. (Courtesy USAMHI.)

On September 1, 1920, General Hospital No. 31 closed its doors, its mission completed, having treated 4,279 patients in the year and nine months it operated. On the day the hospital closed, the Medical Field Service School opened. This school developed new technologies and trained medical personnel in the latest techniques of military medicine. This training also involved field exercises conducted under realistic conditions. (Courtesy USAMHI.)

The post had seen many traumatic events in its time, sometimes at the hand of mankind but other times at the hand of nature. In 1920, a tornado passed near the post carrying away the top floor of the western end of barracks 5, damaging other buildings and toppling many of the large trees on post. (Courtesy USAMHI.)

The tornado uprooted a number of the trees on post and scattered debris over a wide area. Here some of the garrison members examine trees that have been toppled in front of barracks 4. (Courtesy USAMHI.)

Soldiers investigate the toppled trees in front of barracks 4. Crumpled roofing material can be seen at the left. (Courtesy USAMHI.)

Soldiers pause during cleanup operations to pose in front of barracks 4. (Courtesy USAMHI.)

Today the two trees seen at the extreme left and right in the previous view still stand as silent witnesses of the past. (Author's collection.)

Fire was no stranger to the post, having seen a number of fires over the years. In 1922, the dining facility was destroyed by fire resulting in the troops being fed in temporary facilities located on the athletic field until a new mess building was built in 1931 that also incorporated the post exchange, tailor shop, barbershop, and bowling alley. On June 23, 1924, a fire broke out in barracks 3 just after midnight. The old girls' dormitory from the Indian School was doomed. (Courtesy USAMHI.)

At that time, a dance was drawing to a close at the nearby club when the fire was discovered, and many officers pitched in and helped supervise the firefighting efforts while still wearing their formal dress uniforms. The destruction of this barracks caused its residents to be crowded into other buildings until arrangements could be made. The remains of barracks 3 were removed and a tennis court constructed in its place. (Courtesy USAMHI.)

No sign of barracks 3 remains today, and most people who play tennis here have absolutely no idea of the history that has occurred on this small piece of ground. (Author's collection.)

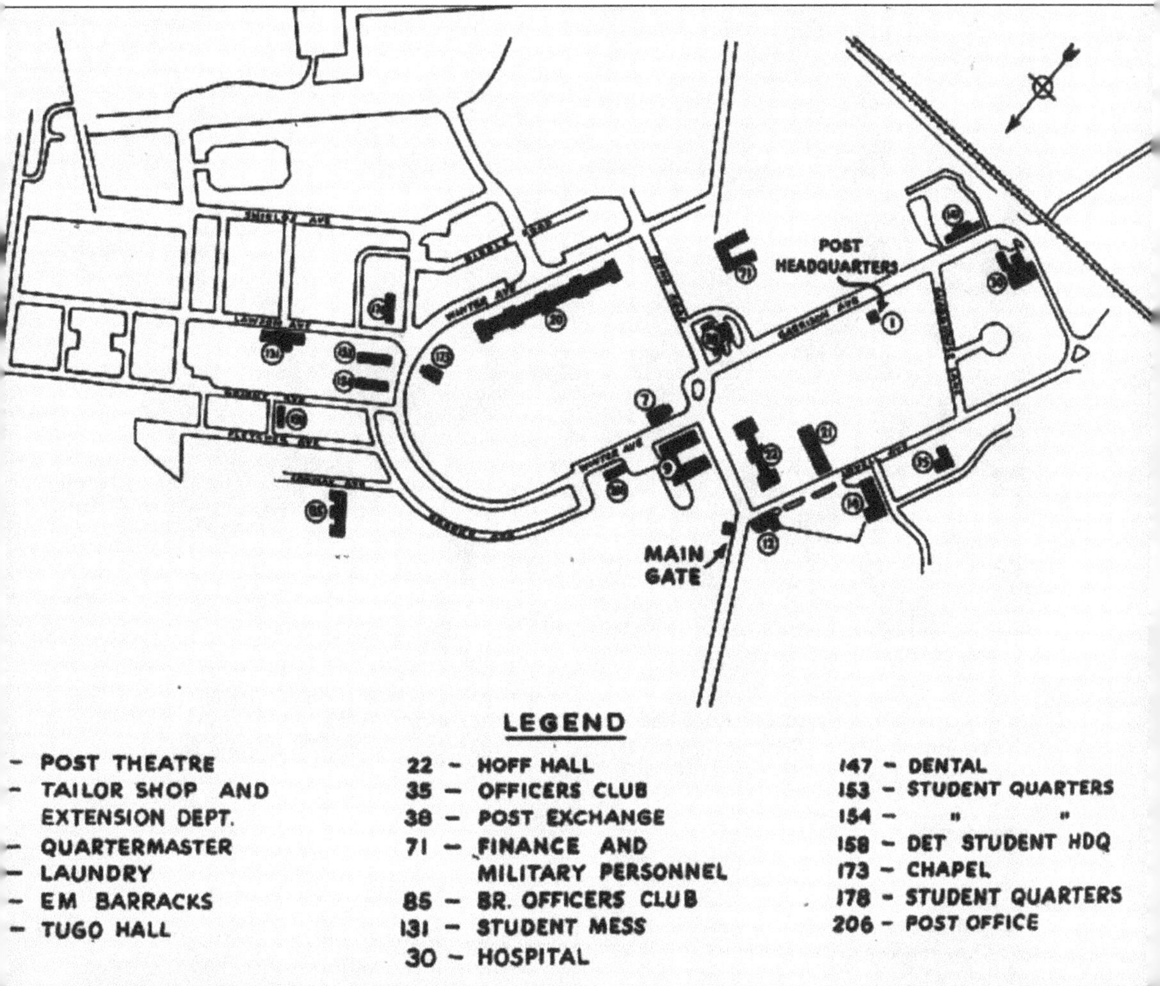

POST
HEADQUARTERS

MAIN
GATE

LEGEND

– POST THEATRE	22 – HOFF HALL	147 – DENTAL
– TAILOR SHOP AND EXTENSION DEPT.	35 – OFFICERS CLUB	153 – STUDENT QUARTERS
	38 – POST EXCHANGE	154 – " "
– QUARTERMASTER	71 – FINANCE AND MILITARY PERSONNEL	158 – DET STUDENT HDQ
– LAUNDRY		173 – CHAPEL
– EM BARRACKS	85 – BR. OFFICERS CLUB	178 – STUDENT QUARTERS
– TUGO HALL	131 – STUDENT MESS	206 – POST OFFICE
	30 – HOSPITAL	

This map shows the medical school facilities and illustrates how the post had expanded out from the original parade ground, seen at right. (Courtesy USAMHI.)

By the 1930s, it became evident that many of the buildings inherited from the Indian School days and before were deteriorating. Here a company of garrison troops forms up on the parade ground in front of barracks 1 that had been in use since its reconstruction in 1864. As a result of the condition of the 19th-century structures, Congress appropriated funds for a general upgrade of the post. (Courtesy USAMHI.)

The old parade ground still served for some functions and ceremonies although the athletic field built by the Native American students was more spacious and accessible. Here troops form up almost exactly where cavalrymen once did the same thing. See images on pages 44 and 45 for comparison. (Courtesy USAMHI.)

The post expanded out from the old quadrangle that had been its heart and soul since 1757, and new facilities were constructed on adjacent property. With war looming in Europe and Asia, the military began increasing troop strength, requiring an expansion of post facilities. A new theater was built adjacent to the athletic field to help replace the auditorium that was lost when barracks 5 was removed. (Courtesy USAMHI.)

After barracks 5 was condemned in 1932 and removed, a new modern barracks was built to replace it adjacent to the athletic field. This barracks opened in 1936 and is known today as Young Hall. (Author's collection.)

In 1935, land was purchased for a new entrance road to replace the old Pratt Avenue entrance. This road was wider and could better accommodate the increased traffic that resulted from the growth of the post. This new entrance was completed and opened in 1936. (Courtesy USAMHI.)

The old cavalry stables had been used as an academic facility by the Indian School and continued in that capacity with the Medical Field Service School, until it burned in December 1928. It was rebuilt and continued to evolve. An addition was eventually built to connect the two front wings together, creating a rectangular building with an open courtyard. Modern views can be seen on page 111. (Courtesy USAMHI.)

A view from the old Washington Hall dormitory, this image shows Young Hall in the distance and troops marching toward the athletic field in 1938. (Courtesy USAMHI.)

This image, taken from the same location as the previous photograph, shows mounted guidon bearers passing the athletic field in 1938. (Courtesy USAMHI.)

Medical Field Service School students pass in review on the athletic field where Native American students once played baseball and football 25 years before. Young Hall is seen beyond. See page 97 for an additional view of Young Hall. (Courtesy USAMHI.)

The growing number of students attending the Medical Field Service School required that many of them be housed in tent encampments on post such as these shown here in 1938. The brick structures housed company orderly rooms and supply room facilities. The long building in the distant center is the post stables. (Courtesy USAMHI.)

The street in the previous image is now a grassy lawn while the lawn to the right in the previous image is now a parking lot. The two brick structures remain today as residences. The water tower and the stables are obscured by foliage. (Courtesy USAMHI.)

This is the dining facility built to replace the old Indian School facility that burned. This facility served all the students housed in the adjacent tent encampment in 1938. See page 115 for a modern image of the building. (Courtesy USAMHI.)

The soldiers and their encampment are gone today, but the old dining facility remains and serves as the post youth center today. (Courtesy USAMHI.)

On April 29, 1939, the commandant was informed that Hoff Hall was unsafe and would need to be replaced. The decision was made to transfer its school functions to the neighboring gymnasium, which was then known as Tugo Hall. Within days, school furnishings and equipment were transferred and Hoff Hall was evacuated. (Courtesy USAMHI.)

On August 1, 1940, working teams began tearing down old barracks 2 that had once housed Native American students and soldiers. (Courtesy USAMHI.)

Within three weeks, there was nothing left of the barracks except its footprint on the land as evidenced by this photograph taken on August 19, 1940. It took 26 working days, 26 men, and 9 trucks per day to remove the old barracks. (Courtesy USAMHI.)

Then a brand-new Hoff Hall began to rise from the memory of barracks 2. (Courtesy USAMHI.)

Using steel beams and limestone, the building was larger and far superior to the old masonry barracks that once occupied this spot. (Courtesy USAMHI.)

The limestone walls go up over the steel beam framing. (Courtesy USAMHI.)

The new Hoff Hall was more expansive and appropriate for the Medical Field Service School. (Courtesy USAMHI.)

In 1942, the country was at war when this image was taken. It shows the guard at the front gate while students gather in front of Hoff Hall. (Courtesy USAMHI.)

This image captures a moment in time when the Carlisle Barracks flagpole stood in front of the commandant's quarters. These quarters stand on the site of Col. John Stanwix's camp in 1757 when he established what would become Carlisle Barracks. They have witnessed much of the history outlined in this book. After the war, the Medical Field Service School was ordered to relocate. During the time the school operated, it trained approximately 30,000 medical officers and corpsmen. It operated throughout World War II and continued until 1946 when the school function was transferred to Fort Sam Houston, Texas. With its departure, the post housed a variety of additional schools from 1946 to 1951. (Courtesy USAMHI.)

Five

THE ARMY WAR COLLEGE AND CARLISLE BARRACKS TODAY

Carlisle Barracks became the home of the U.S. Army War College in 1951 and continued the post's tradition of supporting U.S. Army education. (Author's collection.)

The U.S. Army War College, founded in 1901 at Fort McNair, Washington, D.C., was intended to provide training in leadership, strategic planning, research, and education. During World War II, classes were suspended; however, in 1949, the war college was reopened, reorganized, and brought to Carlisle Barracks in 1951. (Courtesy USAMHI.)

With the war college came a bronze statue of Frederick the Great, 18th-century Prussian king. It had been presented to the college by Kaiser Wilhelm II of Germany as a goodwill gesture and unveiled at the war college in November 1904 by Pres. Theodore Roosevelt. When the school moved to Carlisle, the statue followed in 1954 and was erected on the old parade ground. (Courtesy USAMHI.)

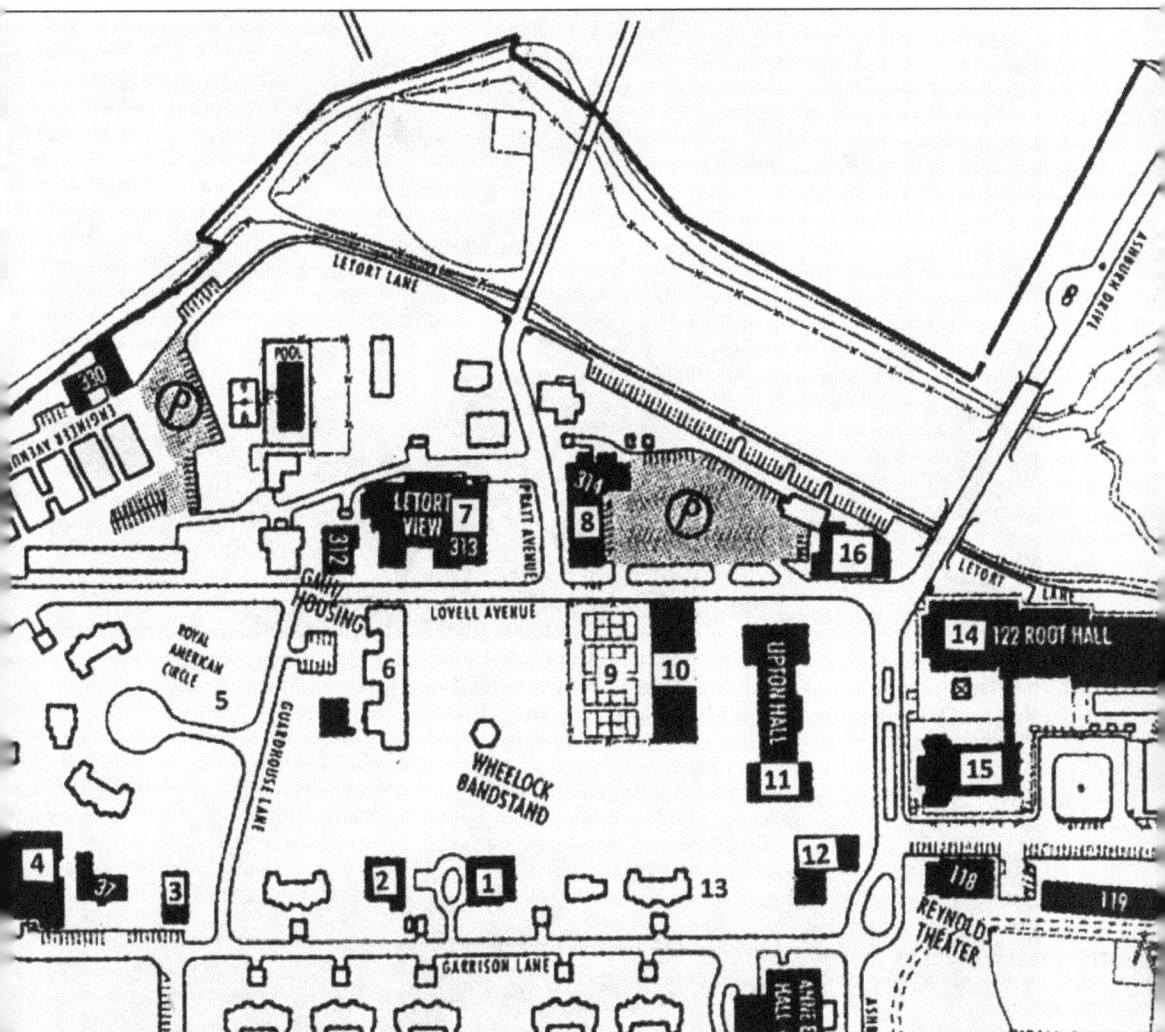

This map shows the old quadrangle of the original post as it appears today. Pictured on the map are the old commandant's quarters known today as quarters 2 (1); old administration and headquarters building known today as quarters 3 (2); Hessian Guard House Interpretive Center (3); Pratt Hall, used as doctors' quarters during the medical school period (4); site of barracks 5 (5); barracks 4, now faculty housing known as Coren Apartments (6); LeTort View Community Center (7); Armstrong Hall, the old post laundry (8); site of barracks 3 (9); Thorpe Gym (10); site of barracks 2 occupied today by Upton Hall (11); Washington Hall, the old Indian School hospital and dormitory, today a guesthouse (12); site of barracks 1 (13); Root Hall, part of the U.S. Army War College (14); site of the old cavalry stables occupied today by new Bliss Hall (15); and old Indian School commissary building (16). (Author's collection.)

This aerial view shows the post much as it appeared when the U.S. Army War College came to Carlisle Barracks. The Medical Field Service School buildings remain and were utilized to support the war college activities. (Courtesy USAMHI.)

Hoff Hall, renamed Root Hall, became the primary war college facility much as it had served the Medical Field Service School. However, the need was seen for a new facility to accommodate the growing requirements for the war college, and in the mid-1960s, construction began on a new Root Hall. This view taken in late 1966 shows the new Root Hall as it nears completion. (Courtesy USAMHI.)

This 1967 aerial view shows Hoff Hall (old Root Hall, now Upton Hall) on the site of barracks 2 seen on the left. At lower right is Washington Hall, a hospital and dormitory for the Indian School, officers' quarters for the medical school, and today a guesthouse. At lower right is the post theater built in the 1930s, which can also be seen on page 97. The refurbished cavalry stable was named Bliss Hall in honor of Col. Tasker Bliss, second commandant of the war college. Behind Bliss Hall is Root Hall, the new home of the U.S. Army War College. (Courtesy USAMHI.)

Another aerial view of old Bliss Hall clearly shows its roots as the old cavalry stables from whence it grew. Root Hall behind Bliss Hall nears completion as the new expanded home of the U.S. Army War College. (Courtesy USAMHI.)

Eventually the old Bliss Hall was taken down and a new facility erected in its place. Today's Bliss Hall bears little resemblance to the cavalry stable that once stood there. (Author's collection.)

The U.S. Army War College complex is shown as seen today. (Courtesy USAMHI.)

Root Hall seen today from the steps of Upton Hall today (old Hoff Hall and Root Hall) remains the home of the U.S. Army War College. The blacksmith shop that served the cavalry units here and the Indian School as well once stood to the left of the steps near where the tree stands at left. Please also see pages 69 and 73. (Courtesy USAMHI.)

The front entrance to Root Hall is pictured as seen today. (Author's collection.)

Collins Hall, home of the Center for Strategic Leadership, is a conference and war-gaming complex that opened in 1994. (Author's collection.)

On May 3, 1930, the post stables were destroyed by fire and replaced in 1931 by new brick stables, seen here. Since horses are no longer a part of the U.S. Army inventory, the stables were converted into offices, shops, and other uses. They remain today as a tangible link to the post's history when it was the home of the U.S. Army's Cavalry School. (Author's collection.)

This brick building today serves as the post youth center. It is an example of the adaptive reuse of numerous buildings on post. During the late 1930s and through World War II, the structure served as a dining facility for troops housed in adjacent wooden barracks. The evidence of four windows on the end facing the camera can be seen where these windows were removed and the openings bricked up. Please also see pages 101 and 102. (Author's collection.)

The LeTort View Community Center as seen today was once the post officers' club. At the very heart of this structure remains the print shop constructed by the Indian School; however, subsequent additions have all but swallowed up this Indian School building. Please also see page 74. (Author's collection.)

In 1938, the Public Works Administration allotted funds for the construction of 9 double sets and 2 single sets of quarters for officers and 14 double sets of quarters for noncommissioned officers, as well as a combination firehouse and guardhouse. These quarters seen here on Forbes Avenue are part of the 14 double sets built for noncommissioned officers. (Author's collection.)

This double set of officers' quarters sits on the site of barracks 1 on the parade ground. (Author's collection.)

Quarters 3, built in 1891 as a vocational training project by Indian School students with local contractor Andrew Wetzel, served as the Indian School administration building. During the General Hospital No. 31 and medical school period, it served as post headquarters. Today it serves as deputy commandant for international affairs quarters. (Author's collection.)

The old commandant's quarters, known today as quarters 2, is the residence for the deputy commandant of the army war college. The structure has been burned and rebuilt, renovated and enlarged. It housed the post commandant and his office in the early years, was the residence for the Indian School superintendent, and served as officers' quarters during General Hospital No. 31. The adjutant's quarters stood in the vacant space to the left. Officers' quarters built in 1938–1939 are located beyond on the left. (Author's collection.)

Barracks 4 is the only barracks from the old post that exists today. It burned in 1857 and again in 1863 and was rebuilt each time. It served as officers' quarters, teachers' quarters, nurses' quarters, and faculty quarters over the years. During the early years of the Indian School, Capt. Richard Pratt's office was on the ground floor room at left. Today the barracks is known as Coren Apartments in honor of Capt. Isaac Coren, commander of the first artillery school at Carlisle Barracks, and houses faculty. (Author's collection.)

Pictured here is the Wheelock Bandstand. The original bandstand was built in 1867. During the medical school period, it was moved to the corner of Pratt Avenue and Lovell Avenue, across from Armstrong Hall on the site of the old dining facility that had burned. That bandstand was eventually removed. In 1980, Wheelock Bandstand was built near the site of the original bandstand and is used today for graduation ceremonies, concerts, and other functions. (Author's collection.)

118

The Hessian powder magazine, built in 1777 by Hessian prisoners as tradition states, served as a powder magazine throughout the Revolution and was converted to a guardhouse during the Cavalry School period, a detention facility during the Indian School period, and a confinement point for General Hospital No. 31 and the medical school until the 1930s when new facilities were constructed. Today the building houses an interpretive center that tells the story of Carlisle Barracks' history. (Author's collection.)

The post athletic field known as Indian Field was constructed by Indian School students who cleared and graded the field to have a facility for the school's growing athletic programs. Glen S. "Pop" Warner coached student athletes here such as football and Olympic legend Jim Thorpe, hall of fame pitcher Charles Bender, and Olympic distance runner Louis Tewanima. The grandstand, built in 1940, replaced the one built by Indian School students. Today it houses the U.S. Army's Physical Fitness Research Institute's assessment and wellness center. (Courtesy USAMHI.)

Building 315 located at Lovell Avenue and Ashburn Drive was built as a commissary for the Indian School but also served General Hospital No. 31, the medical school, and the U.S. Army War College. Today the commissary function is in a more modern facility elsewhere on post in conjunction with the post exchange, and building 315 houses offices that support other U.S. Army War College functions. (Author's collection.)

Hoff Hall was built to replace barracks 2 as an academic facility. In 1951, the war college occupied the building and renamed it Root Hall after Elihu Root. In 1967, the war college moved into the new Root Hall. That year, the USAMHI was organized and occupied a portion of old Root Hall (Hoff Hall), and the building was renamed Upton Hall in honor of Gen. Emory Upton. In 2004, the USAMHI moved to new facilities. Please also see page 106. Today Upton Hall is the post's garrison headquarters. (Author's collection.)

The commandant's quarters moved to this building in 1969. It was built in 1932 by Edwin Barnitz on property adjacent to the post. The property was leased to the U.S. Army in 1951 and purchased in 1959 for bachelor officers' quarters. Tradition says in 1969 the resident officers invited commandant Maj. Gen. George Eckhardt to a Christmas party there, and his wife was so taken with the house that it became the commandant's quarters. (Author's collection.)

Today there are many tangible things on post that connect people to those long-ago days, but perhaps there are none more poignant than the Indian School cemetery where Native American students who passed away while attending the school were buried. (Author's collection.)

The names on each stone may seem curious to some, but each one represents a son or a daughter who had left their homes and families to travel to a strange land to learn from strange people about a different culture in hopes that this knowledge would benefit both cultures. Whether from disease or accident, their lives were cut short. (Author's collection.)

The flowers and mementos that appear on many of the graves today give clear evidence that these young lives are not forgotten, even as the history they represent slips deeper into the past. (Author's collection.)

Each name is a haunting echo from the past, a voice saying "I was here." (Author's collection.)

The old quadrangle is the heart and soul of the post. Its serenity contradicts the tumultuous history that has taken place upon its grounds and within its structures. The post has expanded beyond the old quadrangle that has become lost within the sprawl of the post. The ground where soldiers drilled, where Native American students played, and where history was made, is quiet today; however, the ghosts are everywhere. (Author's collection.)

An aerial view of Carlisle Barracks at the dawn of the 21st century shows its expansion beyond the old quadrangle. Dunham Clinic is at lower center foreground. Indian Field is adjacent to the water tower at upper left. Young Hall is to the right of Indian Field. The Center for Strategic Leadership is above Young Hall, and student housing is to the right of the Center for Strategic Leadership. The post exchange, commissary, and old post stables are at the upper right. (Courtesy USAMHI.)

Here is another aerial view toward the old post. Indian Field is at lower center, and the theater is to the left. Washington Hall is the white L-shaped building at left. Upton Hall is to the right of Washington Hall and Thorpe Gym and to the left of Upton Hall. The tennis court where barracks 3 stood is to the left of the gymnasium. Barracks 4, or Coren Apartments, is at far left. The old commissary can be seen at upper center. Bliss Hall is at upper center, the U.S. Army War College is at center right, and the city of Carlisle can be seen beyond. (Courtesy USAMHI.)

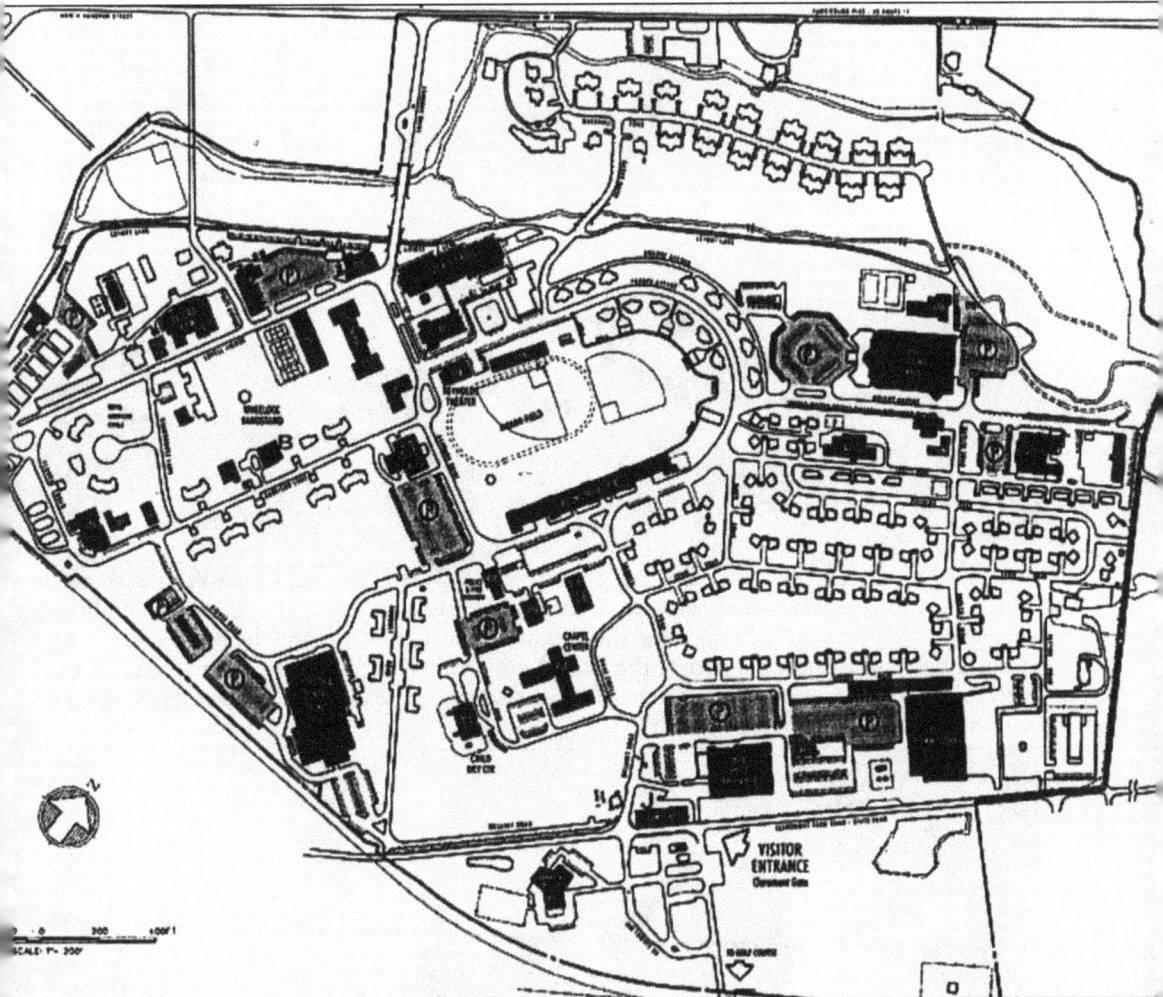

This is a current map of the post of Carlisle Barracks. The old quadrangle, the heart of the post, can be discerned at upper left. (Courtesy USAHEC.)

The U.S. Army Heritage and Education Center is home to the U.S. Army's archive and library dedicated to preserving the history and the heritage of the U.S. Army and the American soldier. Carlisle Barracks has been a part of the U.S. Army's long and distinguished service since the early days of the Revolution. It is fitting that it is also the home of the U.S. Army Heritage and Education Center. (Courtesy USAHEC.)

Frederick the Great stands watch over the old parade ground, the stage upon which much history has played out. (Courtesy USAMHI.)

Carlisle Barracks faces the future but acknowledges its past. Upton Hall, the site of barracks 2, once the home of the Medical Field Service School, the U.S. Army War College, and the military history institute, today houses the garrison headquarters. While the United States flag flies proudly from the post flagpole in front of Root Hall, the flagpole at the garrison headquarters flies the flag of Great Britain in honor of those brave English soldiers who camped upon this ground in 1757 and started a chain of events still being forged today. When Col. John Stanwix and his troops established a camp along the LeTort Spring Run in May 1757, they could not have realized they were planting a seed that would blossom long after they had moved on. Carlisle Barracks is the results of Stanwix's action on that May afternoon. In those intervening years, the post has seen the fervor of war and the stagnation and inactivity of peace. It has seen growth, and it has seen the destruction of war and nature. Over the years, soldiers have come to serve, to learn, and to teach the military profession. Structures were built, enlarged, dismantled, or in some cases, burned, due to accidents or war. Carlisle Barracks has left its mark on those who have been here, and they have left their mark on the post and the country. It has been a crossroads of history as people found their journeys through life bringing them to Carlisle Barracks and then taking them to new challenges. Today people walk the ground where history has taken place. While the people come and go, Carlisle Barracks remains the stage upon which history has happened and is still happening. Those who live and work at Carlisle Barracks today are merely the current players making history upon that stage, while surrounded by the silent witnesses to the history that has been made and the history that is being made. (Author's collection.)

Visit us at
arcadiapublishing.com

www.ingramcontent.com/pod-product-compliance
Lightning Source LLC
Chambersburg PA
CBHW080607110426
42813CB00006B/1428